MAKE, BAKE, CUPCAKE
totally tasty recipes

MAKE, BAKE, CUPCAKE

totally tasty recipes

MAKE, BAKE, CUPCAKE

totally tasty recipes

This edition published by Parragon Books Ltd in 2014
LOVE FOOD is an imprint of Parragon Books Ltd

Parragon Books Ltd
Chartist House
15–17 Trim Street
Bath BA1 1HA, UK
www.parragon.com/lovefood

ISBN 978-1-4723-2696-6

Printed in China

New photography by Ian Garlick
New food styling by Nikki Gee
Illustrations by Charlotte Farmer

Notes for the Reader
This book uses both metric and imperial measurements. Follow the same units of measurement
throughout; do not mix metric and imperial. All spoon measurements are level: teaspoons are
assumed to be 5 ml, and tablespoons are assumed to be 15 ml. Unless otherwise stated, milk is
assumed to be full fat, eggs and individual vegetables are medium, and pepper is freshly ground
black pepper. Unless otherwise stated, all root vegetables should be peeled prior to using.

Garnishes, decorations and serving suggestions are all optional and not necessarily included in the
recipe ingredients or method. The times given are an approximate guide only. Preparation times
differ according to the techniques used by different people and the cooking times may also vary
from those given. Optional ingredients, variations or serving suggestions have not been included in
the time calculations.

Contents

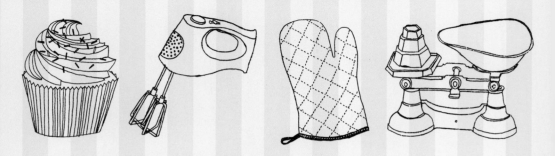

Cake always strikes the perfect note, whether you're baking for a special occasion, or just because you've got a hankering for something sweet. And the cupcake really is the ultimate cake for budding bakers – what's not to love?

Cupcakes themselves are super-simple to make, and easy to add indulgent flavourings to, plus they are the perfect base for all manner of light-as-air scrumptious toppings. Since they're made as individual servings, there's no need to hassle with cutting and serving, and there's never a tussle over the corner piece, since each and every one delivers the perfect ratio of frosting to cake.

A well-baked cupcake is a blank canvas to let your culinary creativity go to town...

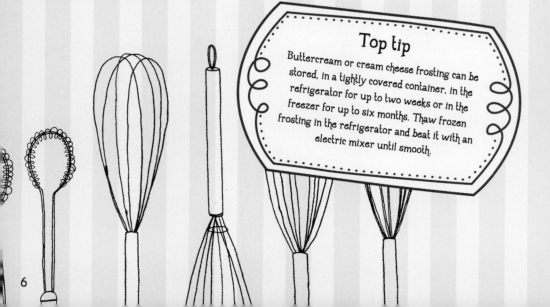

Top tip

Buttercream or cream cheese frosting can be stored, in a tightly covered container, in the refrigerator for up to two weeks or in the freezer for up to six months. Thaw frozen frosting in the refrigerator and beat it with an electric mixer until smooth.

Top tip

Cupcakes topped with buttercream frosting can be stored, covered, at room temperature for up to three days.

Top tip

Unfrosted cupcakes can be frozen, in a single layer in a sealed container, for up to three months. Frost them while they are still frozen, and then defrost them in the refrigerator for several hours.

Cream Tea Cupcakes

makes 10

85 g/3 oz butter, softened

85 g/3 oz caster sugar

1 large egg, lightly beaten

½ tsp vanilla extract

85 g/3 oz self-raising flour

1 tbsp milk

40 g/1½ oz raisins

to decorate

115 g/4 oz strawberries

1 tbsp strawberry jam

115 g/4 oz clotted cream

icing sugar, for dusting

1. Preheat the oven to 190°C/375°F/Gas Mark 5. Put 10 paper cases in a bun tray.

2. Place the butter and caster sugar in a large bowl and beat together until light and fluffy. Gradually beat in the egg and vanilla extract. Sift in the flour and, using a metal spoon, fold gently into the mixture with the milk and raisins.

3. Spoon the mixture into the paper cases. Bake in the preheated oven for 15–20 minutes, or until risen, golden and firm to the touch. Transfer to a wire rack and leave to cool.

4. Use a serrated knife to cut a circle from the top of each cupcake. Hull and slice the strawberries, then gently mix together the strawberries and jam and divide among the cupcakes. Top each with a small dollop of clotted cream. Replace the cupcake tops and dust with icing sugar.

2

4

4

Black Forest Cupcakes

makes 12

1 tsp lemon juice

4 tbsp milk

150 g/5½ oz self-raising flour

½ tsp bicarbonate of soda

2 eggs, lightly beaten

55 g/2 oz butter, softened

115 g/4 oz soft light brown sugar

1 tbsp cocoa powder

85 g/3 oz plain chocolate, melted

25 g/1 oz dried and sweetened
sour cherries, chopped

to decorate

2 tbsp cherry liqueur (optional)

150 ml/5 fl oz double cream,
softly whipped

5 tbsp cherry jam

cocoa powder, for dusting

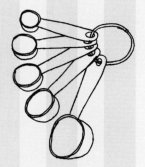

1. Preheat the oven to 180°C/350°F/Gas Mark 4.
Put 12 paper cases in a muffin tray.

2. Add the lemon juice to the milk and leave for
10 minutes – the milk will curdle a little.

3. Meanwhile, sift the flour and bicarbonate of
soda into a large bowl. Add the eggs, butter, brown
sugar and milk mixture and, using an electric
mixer, beat until smooth. Sift in the cocoa powder
and beat in. Fold in the melted chocolate and sour
cherries.

4. Spoon the mixture into the paper cases. Bake
in the preheated oven for 20–25 minutes, or until
risen and firm to the touch. Transfer to a wire rack
and leave to cool.

5. Cut a circle from the top of each cupcake.
Sprinkle the cupcakes with the cherry liqueur, if
using. Spoon the whipped cream onto the centres
and top with a small spoonful of jam. Gently
replace the cupcake tops and dust lightly with
cocoa powder.

Top tip
Store the cupcakes, undecorated, for up to three days in an airtight container and eat on the day of decorating.

2

2

3

Lemon Meringue Cupcakes

makes 4

85 g/3 oz butter, softened,
plus extra for greasing

85 g/3 oz caster sugar

finely grated rind and juice of
½ lemon

1 large egg

85 g/3 oz self-raising flour

2 tbsp lemon curd

meringue

2 egg whites

115 g/4 oz caster sugar

1. Preheat the oven to 190°C/375°F/Gas Mark 5.
Grease 4 x 200-ml/7-fl oz ovenproof ramekins.

2. Place the butter, caster sugar and lemon rind
in a large bowl and beat together until light and
fluffy. Gradually beat in the egg. Sift in the flour
and, using a metal spoon, fold into the mixture
with the lemon juice.

3. Spoon the mixture into the ramekins. Put the
ramekins on a baking sheet. Bake in the preheated
oven for 15 minutes, or until risen, golden and
firm to the touch.

4. While the cupcakes are baking, make the
meringue. Put the egg whites in a clean, grease-
free bowl and, using an electric mixer, whisk until
stiff peaks are formed. Gradually whisk in the
caster sugar until glossy.

5. Spread the lemon curd over the hot cupcakes,
then swirl over the meringue. Return the
cupcakes to the oven for 4–5 minutes, until the
meringue is golden. Serve immediately.

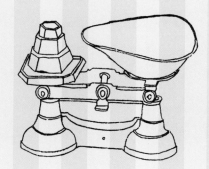

Frosted Berry Cupcakes

makes 12

115 g/4 oz butter, softened

115 g/4 oz caster sugar

2 tsp orange flower water

2 large eggs, lightly beaten

55 g/2 oz ground almonds

115 g/4 oz self-raising flour

2 tbsp milk

frosting

300 g/10¼ oz mascarpone cheese

85 g/3 oz caster sugar

4 tbsp orange juice

to decorate

280 g/10 oz mixed berries

1 large egg white, beaten

caster sugar, for sprinkling

several fresh mint leaves

1. Preheat the oven to 180°C/350°F/Gas Mark 4. Put 12 paper cases in a bun tray.

2. Place the butter, caster sugar and orange flower water in a large bowl and beat together until light and fluffy. Gradually beat in the eggs. Stir in the ground almonds. Sift in the flour and, using a metal spoon, fold in gently with the milk.

3. Spoon the mixture into the paper cases. Bake in the preheated oven for 15–20 minutes, until risen, golden and firm to the touch. Transfer to a wire rack and leave to cool.

4. To make the decorations, brush the mixed berries and mint leaves with egg white. Spinkle generously with caster sugar and set aside to dry.

5. To make the frosting, put the mascarpone, caster
sugar and orange juice in a bowl and beat together until smooth.

6. Swirl the frosting over the top of the cupcakes and arrange the sugar-frosted berries and mint leaves on top.

Gooey Chocolate & Cream Cheese Cupcakes

makes 12

175 g/6 oz plain flour

20 g/¾ oz cocoa powder

¾ tsp bicarbonate of soda

200 g/7 oz caster sugar

50 ml/2 fl oz sunflower oil

175 ml/6 fl oz water

2 tsp white vinegar

½ tsp vanilla extract

150 g/5½ oz full-fat cream cheese

1 egg, lightly beaten

100 g/3½ oz plain chocolate, broken into pieces

1. Preheat the oven to 180°C/350°F/Gas Mark 4. Put 12 paper cases in a bun tray.

2. Sift the flour, cocoa powder and bicarbonate of soda into a large bowl. Stir 150 g/5½ oz of the caster sugar into the flour mixture. Add the oil, water, vinegar and vanilla extract and stir well until combined.

3. Place the remaining caster sugar, the cream cheese and egg in a large bowl and beat together until well mixed.

4. Put the chocolate in a heatproof bowl set over a saucepan of gently simmering water and heat until melted. Set aside to cool for 5 minutes, stirring occasionally, then stir the chocolate into the cream cheese mixture.

5. Spoon the cake mixture into the paper cases and top each with a spoonful of the cream cheese mixture. Bake in the preheated oven for 20–25 minutes, or until risen and firm to the touch.

6. Transfer to a wire rack and leave to cool.

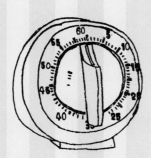

Coffee Fudge Cupcakes

makes 28

175 g/6 oz plain flour

1 tbsp baking powder

175 g/6 oz butter, softened

175 g/6 oz caster sugar

3 eggs, lightly beaten

1 tsp coffee extract

2 tbsp milk

28 chocolate-covered coffee beans, to decorate

frosting

55 g/2 oz unsalted butter, softened

115 g/4 oz light muscovado sugar

2 tbsp single cream or milk

½ tsp coffee extract

400 g/14 oz icing sugar

1. Preheat the oven to 190°C/375°F/Gas Mark 5. Put 28 paper cases in bun trays.

2. Sift the flour and baking powder into a large bowl. Add the butter, caster sugar, eggs and coffee extract and, using an electric mixer, beat together until smooth. Beat in the milk.

3. Spoon the mixture into the paper cases. Bake in the preheated oven for 15–20 minutes, or until risen, golden and firm to the touch. Transfer to a wire rack and leave to cool.

4. To make the frosting, place the butter, muscovado sugar, cream and coffee extract in a saucepan over a medium heat and stir until melted and smooth. Bring to the boil and boil, stirring, for 2 minutes. Remove from the heat and sift in the icing sugar. Stir the frosting until smooth and thick.

5. Spoon the frosting into a piping bag fitted with a large star nozzle. Pipe a swirl of frosting on top of each cupcake and top with a chocolate-covered coffee bean.

Tiramisu Cupcakes

makes 12

115 g/4 oz self-raising flour

½ tsp baking powder

115 g/4 oz butter, softened

115 g/4 oz soft light brown sugar

2 eggs, lightly beaten

2 tbsp finely grated plain
chocolate, to decorate

coffee syrup

2 tsp instant coffee granules

25 g/1 oz icing sugar

4 tbsp water

frosting

225 g/8 oz mascarpone cheese

85 g/3 oz caster sugar

2 tbsp Marsala or sweet sherry

1. Preheat the oven to 180°C/350°F/Gas Mark 4. Put 12 paper cases in a bun tray.

2. Sift the flour and baking powder into a large bowl. Add the butter, brown sugar and eggs and, using an electric mixer, beat together until smooth.

3. Spoon the mixture into the paper cases. Bake in the preheated oven for 15–20 minutes, or until risen, golden and firm to the touch.

4. Meanwhile, make the coffee syrup. Put the coffee granules, icing sugar and water in a pan and heat gently, stirring, until the coffee and sugar have dissolved. Boil for 1 minute, then leave to cool for 10 minutes.

5. Prick the tops of the warm cupcakes all over with a skewer and brush with the coffee syrup. Transfer to a wire rack and leave to cool.

6. To make the frosting, put the mascarpone, caster sugar and Marsala in a bowl and beat together until smooth. Spread over the top of the cupcakes. Using a star stencil, carefully sprinkle the grated chocolate over the frosting.

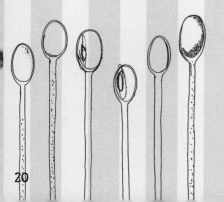

2

5

6

Devil's Food Cupcakes

makes 18

115 g/4 oz plain flour

½ tsp bicarbonate of soda

25 g/1 oz cocoa powder

50 g/1¾ oz butter, softened

115 g/4 oz soft dark brown sugar

2 large eggs, lightly beaten

125 ml/4 fl oz soured cream

chocolate caraque,
to decorate

frosting

125 g/4¼ oz plain chocolate,
broken into pieces

2 tbsp caster sugar

150 ml/5 fl oz soured cream

1. Preheat the oven to 180°C/350°F/Gas Mark 4. Put 18 paper cases in bun trays.

2. Sift the flour, bicarbonate of soda and cocoa powder into a large bowl. Add the butter, brown sugar and eggs and, using an electric mixer, beat together until smooth. Fold in the soured cream.

3. Spoon the mixture into the paper cases. Bake in the preheated oven for 20 minutes, or until risen and firm to the touch. Transfer to a wire rack and leave to cool.

4. To make the frosting, place the chocolate in a heatproof bowl set over a saucepan of gently simmering water and heat until melted, stirring occasionally. Remove from the heat and leave to cool slightly, then beat in the caster sugar and soured cream until combined.

5. Spread the frosting over the tops of the cupcakes and decorate with chocolate caraque. Leave to set.

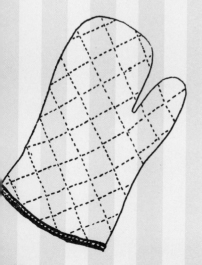

2

4

5

White Chocolate
& Rose Cupcakes

makes 12

115 g/4 oz butter, softened

115 g/4 oz caster sugar

1 tsp rose water

2 eggs, lightly beaten

115 g/4 oz self-raising flour

55 g/2 oz white chocolate, grated

frosting

115 g/4 oz white chocolate, broken into pieces

2 tbsp milk

175 g/6 oz full-fat cream cheese

25 g/1 oz icing sugar

to decorate

24 rose petals

1 egg white, beaten

caster sugar, for sprinkling

1. Preheat the oven to 180°C/350°F/Gas Mark 4. Put 12 paper cases in a bun tray.

2. Place the butter, caster sugar and rose water in a large bowl and beat together until light and fluffy. Gradually beat in the eggs. Sift in the flour and, using a metal spoon, fold in gently. Fold in the grated chocolate.

3. Spoon the mixture into the paper cases. Bake in the preheated oven for 15–20 minutes, or until risen, golden and firm to the touch. Transfer to a wire rack and leave to cool.

4. To make the frosting, place the chocolate and milk in a heatproof bowl set over a saucepan of simmering water and leave until melted. Remove from the heat and stir until smooth. Leave to cool for 30 minutes. Put the cream cheese in a separate bowl, sift in the icing sugar and beat together until smooth and creamy. Fold in the melted chocolate. Chill in the refrigerator for 1 hour.

5. To make the decorations, brush the rose petals with egg white and sprinkle generously with caster sugar. Set aside to dry.

6. Swirl the frosting over the top of the cupcakes. Decorate with sugar-frosted rose petals.

3

4

5

Carrot Cake Cupcakes

makes 12

55 g/2 oz walnuts

300 g/10½ oz carrots

175 g/6 oz butter, softened

115 g/4 oz caster sugar

2 eggs, lightly beaten

2 tbsp orange juice

grated rind of ½ orange

175 g/6 oz self-raising flour

1 tsp ground cinnamon

12 walnut halves,
to decorate

frosting

115 g/4 oz full-fat cream cheese

1 tbsp orange juice

225 g/8 oz icing sugar

1. Preheat the oven to 180°C/350°F/Gas Mark 4. Put 12 paper cases in a bun tray.

2. Finely chop the walnuts and then roughly grate the carrots.

3. Place the butter and caster sugar in a large bowl and beat together until light and fluffy. Gradually beat in the eggs. Fold in the carrots, chopped walnuts, orange juice and orange rind. Sift in the flour and cinnamon and, using a metal spoon, fold in gently.

4. Spoon the mixture into the paper cases. Bake in the preheated oven for 15–20 minutes, or until risen, golden and firm to the touch. Transfer to a wire rack and leave to cool.

5. To make the frosting, put the cream cheese and orange juice in a bowl. Sift in the icing sugar and beat until fluffy. Spread the frosting over the cupcakes and top each with a walnut half.

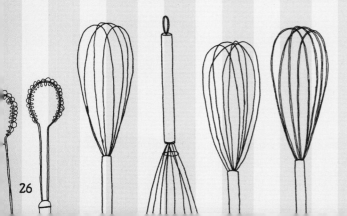

Top tip

Swap full fat cream cheese for a reduced fat version. It still has the tasty tang of traditional carrot cake frosting.

2

2

3

Macadamia & Maple Cupcakes

makes 10

85 g/3 oz butter, softened

55 g/2 oz soft light brown sugar

2 tbsp maple syrup

1 large egg, lightly beaten

85 g/3 oz self-raising flour

55 g/2 oz macadamia nuts, chopped

1 tbsp milk

frosting

25 g/1 oz unsalted butter, softened

2 tbsp maple syrup

85 g/3 oz icing sugar

85 g/3 oz cream cheese

1. Preheat the oven to 190°C/375°F/Gas Mark 5. Put 10 paper cases in a bun tray.

2. Place the butter, brown sugar and maple syrup in a large bowl and beat together until light and fluffy. Gradually beat in the egg. Sift in the flour and, using a metal spoon, fold into the mixture with the nuts and milk.

3. Spoon the mixture into the paper cases. Bake in the preheated oven for 20 minutes, or until risen, golden and firm to the touch. Transfer to a wire rack and leave to cool.

4. To make the frosting, beat the butter and maple syrup together until smooth. Sift in the icing sugar and beat in thoroughly. Gently beat in the cream cheese. Swirl the frosting on top of the cupcakes.

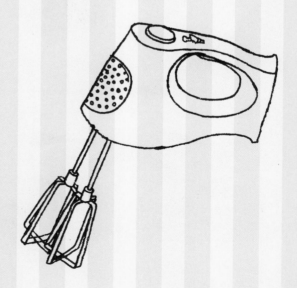

Apple Streusel Cupcakes

makes 14

¼ tsp bicarbonate of soda

280 g/10 oz apple sauce

55 g/2 oz butter, softened

85 g/3 oz demerara sugar

1 large egg

175 g/6 oz self-raising flour

½ tsp ground cinnamon

½ tsp freshly grated nutmeg

topping

50 g/1¾ oz plain flour

50 g/1¾ oz demerara sugar

¼ tsp ground cinnamon

freshly grated nutmeg, to taste

35 g/1¼ oz butter

1. Preheat the oven to 180°C/350°F/Gas Mark 4. Put 14 paper cases in bun trays.

2. To make the topping, put the flour, demerara sugar, cinnamon and nutmeg, to taste, in a bowl. Cut the butter into small pieces, then add to the bowl and rub it in with your fingertips until the mixture resembles fine breadcrumbs. Set aside.

3. Add the bicarbonate of soda to the apple sauce and stir until dissolved.

4. Place the butter and demerara sugar in a large bowl and beat together until light and fluffy. Lightly beat the egg in a separate bowl, then add to the butter mixture. Sift in the flour, cinnamon and nutmeg and fold into the mixture, adding the apple sauce a spoonful at a time.

5. Spoon the mixture into the paper cases. Scatter the topping over the cupcakes and press down gently. Bake in the preheated oven for 20 minutes, or until risen, golden and firm to the touch. Transfer to a wire rack and leave to cool.

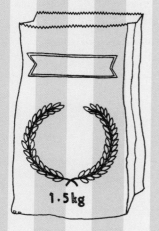

1.5kg

Pistachio Cupcakes

makes 16

85 g/3 oz unsalted pistachio nuts

115 g/4 oz butter, softened

140 g/5 oz caster sugar

140 g/5 oz self-raising flour

2 eggs, lightly beaten

4 tbsp Greek-style yogurt

1 tbsp chopped pistachio nuts,
to decorate

frosting

115 g/4 oz unsalted butter,
softened

2 tbsp lime juice cordial

green food colouring (optional)

200 g/7 oz icing sugar

1. Preheat the oven to 180°C/350°F/Gas Mark 4. Put 16 paper cases in bun trays.

2. Put the pistachio nuts in a food processor or blender and process for a few seconds until finely ground. Transfer the ground nuts to a large bowl and add the butter, caster sugar, flour, eggs and yogurt. Using an electric mixer, beat everything together until smooth.

3. Spoon the mixture into the paper cases. Bake in the preheated oven for 20–25 minutes, or until risen, golden and firm to the touch. Transfer to a wire rack and leave to cool.

4. To make the frosting, put the butter, lime cordial and a little green food colouring, if using, in a bowl and beat until fluffy. Sift in the icing sugar and beat until smooth. Spoon the frosting into a piping bag fitted with a large star nozzle. Pipe a swirl of frosting on top of each cupcake and decorate with the chopped pistachio nuts.

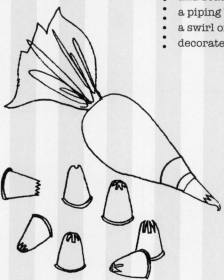

Lemon Polenta Cupcakes

makes 14

115 g/4 oz butter, softened

115 g/4 oz golden caster sugar

finely grated rind and juice of
½ lemon

2 eggs, lightly beaten

55 g/2 oz plain flour

1 tsp baking powder

55 g/2 oz quick-cook polenta

14 crystallized violets,
to decorate

frosting

150 g/5½ oz mascarpone cheese

25 g/1 oz icing sugar

2 tsp finely grated lemon rind

1. Preheat the oven to 180°C/350°F/Gas Mark 4. Put 14 paper cases in bun trays.

2. Place the butter and caster sugar in a large bowl and beat together until light and fluffy. Beat in the lemon rind and juice. Gradually beat in the eggs. Sift in the flour and baking powder and, using a metal spoon, fold gently into the mixture with the polenta.

3. Spoon the mixture into the paper cases. Bake in the preheated oven for 20 minutes, or until risen, golden and firm to the touch. Transfer to a wire rack and leave to cool.

4. To make the frosting, beat the mascarpone until smooth. Sift in the icing sugar, add the lemon rind and beat together until well mixed. Swirl the frosting over the cupcakes and decorate with crystallized violets.

Red Velvet Cupcakes

makes 12

140 g/5 oz plain flour

1 tsp bicarbonate of soda

2 tbsp cocoa powder

115 g/4 oz butter, softened

140 g/5 oz caster sugar

1 large egg, lightly beaten

125 ml/4 fl oz buttermilk

1 tsp vanilla extract

1 tbsp red food colouring

frosting

140 g/5 oz full-fat cream cheese

85 g/3 oz unsalted butter, softened

280 g/10 oz icing sugar

to decorate

55 g/2 oz granulated sugar

red food colouring paste

1. Preheat the oven to 180°C/350°F/Gas Mark 4. Put 12 paper cases in a bun tray.

2. Sift together the flour, bicarbonate of soda and cocoa powder. Place the butter and caster sugar in a separate large bowl and beat together until light and fluffy. Gradually beat in the egg and half the flour mixture. Beat in the buttermilk, vanilla extract and red food colouring. Fold in the remaining flour mixture.

3. Spoon the mixture into the paper cases. Bake the cupcakes in the preheated oven for 15–20 minutes, or until risen and firm to the touch. Transfer to a wire rack and leave to cool.

4. To make the frosting, put the cream cheese and butter in a bowl and blend together with a spatula. Sift in the icing sugar and beat until smooth and creamy.

5. Place the granulated sugar and a little red food colouring paste in a plastic bag. Rub the bag between your fingers and thumb until well mixed. Swirl the frosting on the top of the cupcakes and sprinkle with the coloured sugar.

2

4

5

Gingerbread Cupcakes

makes 30

175 g/6 oz plain flour

1 tbsp baking powder

2 tsp ground ginger

1 tsp ground cinnamon

175 g/6 oz butter, softened

175 g/6 oz dark muscovado sugar

3 eggs, lightly beaten

1 tsp vanilla extract

chopped crystallized ginger, to decorate

frosting

85 g/3 oz unsalted butter, softened

3 tbsp orange juice

150 g/5½ oz icing sugar

1. Preheat the oven to 190°C/375°F/Gas Mark 5. Put 30 paper cases into mini bun trays.

2. Sift the flour, baking powder, ground ginger and cinnamon into a large bowl. Add the butter, muscovado sugar, eggs and vanilla extract and, using an electric mixer, beat together until smooth.

3. Spoon the mixture into the paper cases. Bake in the preheated oven for 15-20 minutes, or until risen, golden and firm to the touch. Transfer to a wire rack and leave to cool.

4. To make the frosting, place the butter and orange juice in a bowl and beat with an electric mixer until smooth. Sift in the icing sugar and continue beating until light and fluffy. Spoon the frosting into a piping bag fitted with a star nozzle. Pipe a little swirl of frosting on top of each cupcake and scatter over the crystallized ginger.

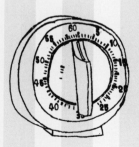

Butterscotch Cupcakes

makes 28

175 g/6 oz plain flour

1 tbsp baking powder

175 g/6 oz butter, softened

175 g/6 oz light muscovado sugar

1 tsp vanilla extract

3 eggs

topping

2 tbsp golden syrup

25 g/1 oz unsalted butter

2 tbsp light muscovado sugar

1. Preheat the oven to 190°C/375°F/Gas Mark 5. Put 28 paper cases into bun trays.

2. Sift the flour and baking powder into a large bowl. Add the butter, muscovado sugar, vanilla extract and eggs and, using an electric mixer, beat together until smooth.

3. Spoon the mixture into the paper cases. Bake in the preheated oven for 15-20 minutes, or until risen, golden and firm to the touch. Transfer to a wire rack and leave to cool.

4. To make the topping, place the golden syrup, butter and muscovado sugar in a small pan and heat gently, stirring, until the sugar dissolves. Bring to the boil and cook, stirring, for about 1 minute. Drizzle over the cupcakes and leave to set.

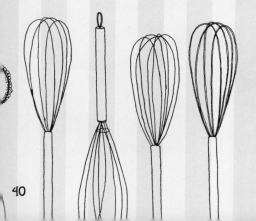

Chocolate Brownie Cupcakes

makes 12

225 g/8 oz plain chocolate, broken into pieces

85 g/3 oz butter, softened

2 large eggs, lightly beaten

200 g/7 oz soft dark brown sugar

1 tsp vanilla extract

140 g/5 oz plain flour

75g/2¾ oz walnuts, finely chopped

1. Preheat the oven to 180°C/350°F/Gas Mark 4. Put 12 paper cases in a bun tray.

2. Place the chocolate and butter in a saucepan and heat gently, stirring constantly, until melted. Remove from the heat and stir until smooth. Leave to cool slightly.

3. Place the eggs and brown sugar in a large bowl and beat together, then add the vanilla extract. Sift in the flour and fold in gently, then stir in the melted chocolate mixture until combined. Stir in the chopped walnuts.

4. Spoon the mixture into the paper cases. Bake in the preheated oven for 30 minutes, or until firm to the touch but still slightly moist in the centre. Transfer to a wire rack and leave to cool.

Top tip

Instead of using paper cases, simply grease the cups of a bun tray with butter and pour the brownie mixture straight in!

2

3

3

Chocolate Paradise Cupcakes

makes 16

85 g/3 oz plain chocolate, broken into pieces

50 ml/2 fl oz milk

1 tbsp cocoa powder

115 g/4 oz butter, softened

115 g/4 oz dark muscovado sugar

2 large eggs, lightly beaten

3 tbsp soured cream

175 g/6 oz plain flour

½ tsp bicarbonate of soda

topping

115 g/4 oz mini white marshmallows

3 tbsp milk

300 ml/10 fl oz double cream

55 g/2 oz desiccated coconut

55 g/2 oz plain chocolate, broken into pieces

1. Preheat the oven to 180°C/350°F/Gas Mark 4. Put 16 paper cases in bun trays.

2. Place the chocolate, milk and cocoa powder in a heatproof bowl set over a saucepan of simmering water and leave until the chocolate has melted. Remove from the heat and stir until smooth.

3. Place the butter and muscovado sugar in a large bowl and beat together until light and fluffy. Gradually beat in the eggs, then beat in the melted chocolate mixture and soured cream. Sift in the flour and bicarbonate of soda and, using a metal spoon, fold in gently.

4. Spoon the mixture into the paper cases. Bake in the preheated oven for 18–20 minutes, or until risen and firm to the touch. Transfer to a wire rack and leave to cool.

5. Place the marshmallows and milk in a heatproof bowl set over a saucepan of simmering water. Leave until the marshmallows have melted, stirring occasionally. Remove from the heat and leave to cool. Whip the cream until holding firm peaks, then fold into the marshmallow mixture with 35 g/1¼ oz of the desiccated coconut. Cover and chill in the refrigerator for 30 minutes.

6. Spread the frosting on top of the cupcakes. Sprinkle over the remaining desiccated coconut. Put the chocolate in a heatproof bowl set over a saucepan of gently simmering water and heat until melted. Then spoon the chocolate into a small paper piping bag, snip off the end and pipe zig-zag lines over the top of each cupcake. Leave to set.

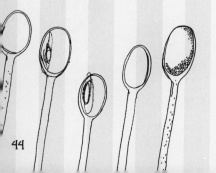

44

45

Hummingbird Cupcakes

makes 12

2 canned pineapple rings,
drained

25 g/1 oz pecan nuts,
plus 6 to decorate

150 g/5½ oz plain flour

¾ tsp bicarbonate of soda

1 tsp ground cinnamon

125 g/4½ oz soft light brown
sugar

2 eggs, lightly beaten

100 ml/3½ fl oz sunflower oil

1 ripe banana, mashed

frosting

140 g/5 oz full-fat
cream cheese

70 g/2½ oz unsalted butter,
softened

1 tsp vanilla extract

280 g/10 oz icing sugar

1. Finely chop the pineapple rings and pecan nuts.

2. Preheat the oven to 180°C/350°F/Gas Mark 4.
Put 12 paper cases in a bun tray.

3. Sift the flour, bicarbonate of soda and cinnamon
into a bowl and stir in the brown sugar. Add the
eggs, oil, banana, pineapple and chopped pecan
nuts and mix thoroughly.

4. Spoon the mixture into the paper cases. Bake
in the preheated oven for 15–20 minutes, or until
risen, golden and firm to the touch. Transfer to a
wire rack and leave to cool.

5. To make the frosting, put the cream cheese,
butter and vanilla extract in a bowl and blend
together with a spatula. Sift in the icing sugar and
beat until smooth and creamy.

6. Spoon the frosting into a piping bag fitted with
a large star nozzle and pipe a wavy line of frosting
on top of each cupcake. Cut the 6 remaining pecan
nuts in half and use to decorate.

Toffee Apple Cupcakes

makes 16

2 eating apples

1 tbsp lemon juice

250 g/9 oz plain flour

2 tsp baking powder

1½ tsp ground cinnamon

70 g/2½ oz light muscovado sugar

55 g/2 oz butter, melted, plus extra for greasing

100 ml/3½ fl oz milk

100 ml/3½ fl oz apple juice

1 egg, lightly beaten

toffee sauce

2 tbsp double cream

40 g/1½ oz light muscovado sugar

15 g/½ oz butter

1. Preheat the oven to 200°C/400°F/Gas Mark 6. Grease 16 holes in 2 bun trays.

2. Roughly grate 1 of the apples. Cut the remaining apple into 5-mm/¼-inch thick slices and toss in the lemon juice. Sift the flour, baking powder and cinnamon into a large bowl, then stir in the muscovado sugar and grated apple.

3. Combine the melted butter with the milk, apple juice and egg. Stir the liquid ingredients into the dry ingredients, mixing lightly until just combined.

4. Spoon the mixture into the prepared bun tray and arrange 2 of the apple slices on top of each cupcake. Bake in the preheated oven for 15–20 minutes, or until risen, golden and firm to the touch. Transfer to a wire rack and leave to cool.

5. To make the toffee sauce, place all the ingredients in a small pan and heat, stirring, until the sugar is dissolved. Increase the heat and boil rapidly for 2 minutes, or until slightly thickened and syrupy. Cool slightly, then drizzle over the cupcakes and leave to set.

Chocolate Florentine Cupcakes

makes 12

55 g/2 oz plain chocolate, broken into pieces

85 g/3 oz butter, softened

1 tbsp golden syrup

55 g/2 oz soft light brown sugar

115 g/4 oz self-raising flour

1 large egg, lightly beaten

topping

40 g/1½ oz glacé cherries, chopped

25 g/1 oz flaked almonds

1 tbsp raisins

1 tbsp golden syrup

1. Preheat the oven to 190°C/375°F/Gas Mark 5. Put 12 paper cases in a bun tray.

2. Put the chocolate, butter, golden syrup and brown sugar in a saucepan and heat gently, stirring occasionally, until just melted. Leave to cool for 2 minutes.

3. Sift the flour into a large bowl and pour in the chocolate mixture. Add the egg and beat until thoroughly blended.

4. Spoon the mixture into the paper cases. Mix together the topping ingredients and gently spoon a little of the mixture on top of each cupcake.

5. Bake in the preheated oven for 15–20 minutes, or until risen and firm to the touch. Transfer to a wire rack and leave to cool.

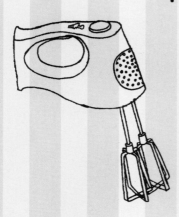

Marbled Chocolate Cupcakes

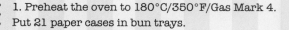

makes 21

3 eggs

175 g/6 oz self-raising flour

175 g/6 oz butter, softened

175 g/6 oz caster sugar

2 tbsp milk

55 g/2 oz plain chocolate,
broken into pieces

1. Preheat the oven to 180°C/350°F/Gas Mark 4.
Put 21 paper cases in bun trays.

2. Beat the eggs together with a whisk in a small
bowl. Sift the flour into a separate large bowl. Add
the butter, caster sugar, eggs and milk and, using
an electric mixer, beat together until smooth.

3. Put the chocolate in a heatproof bowl set over
a saucepan of gently simmering water and heat
until melted.

4. Divide the cake mixture between 2 bowls. Add
the melted chocolate to 1 of the bowls and stir
until well mixed. Place alternate teaspoonfuls of
the mixtures into the paper cases.

5. Bake in the preheated oven for 20 minutes, or
until risen and firm to the touch. Transfer to a
wire rack and leave to cool.

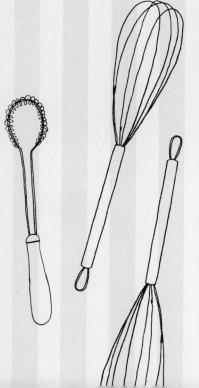

Pink & White Cupcakes

makes 16

115 g/4 oz self-raising flour

1 tsp baking powder

115 g/4 oz butter, softened

115 g/4 oz caster sugar

2 eggs, lightly beaten

1 tbsp milk

red food colouring (optional)

topping

1 egg white

175 g/6 oz caster sugar

2 tbsp hot water

large pinch of cream of tartar

2 tbsp raspberry jam

2 tbsp lightly toasted desiccated coconut

1. Preheat the oven to 180°C/350°F/Gas Mark 4. Put 16 paper cases in bun trays.

2. Sift the flour and baking powder into a large bowl. Add the butter, caster sugar and eggs and, using an electric mixer, beat together until smooth. Mix together the milk and a little red food colouring, if using, and beat into the mixture until evenly blended.

3. Spoon the mixture into the paper cases. Bake in the preheated oven for 20 minutes, or until risen, golden and firm to the touch. Transfer to a wire rack and leave to cool.

4. Put the egg white, caster sugar, water and cream of tartar in a heatproof bowl set over a saucepan of simmering water. Using an electric mixer, beat for 5-6 minutes, until the mixture is thick and holds soft peaks when the whisk is lifted.

5. Spread a layer of jam over each cupcake, then swirl over the frosting. Sprinkle with the desiccated coconut.

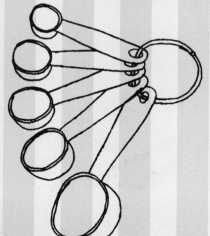

Caramel Cupcakes

makes 12

85 g/3 oz butter, softened

55 g/2 oz soft dark brown sugar

1 tbsp golden syrup

1 large egg, lightly beaten

100 g/3½ oz self-raising flour

1 tsp freshly grated nutmeg

2 tbsp milk

topping

115 g/4 oz soft light brown sugar

1 small egg white

1 tbsp hot water

pinch of cream of tartar

1. Preheat the oven to 180°C/350°F/Gas Mark 4. Put 12 paper cases in a bun tray.

2. Place the butter, dark brown sugar and golden syrup in a large bowl and beat together until light and fluffy. Gradually beat in the egg. Sift in the flour and nutmeg and, using a metal spoon, fold gently into the mixture with the milk.

3. Spoon the mixture into the paper cases. Bake in the preheated oven for 15–20 minutes, or until risen, golden and firm to the touch. Transfer to a wire rack and leave to cool.

4. To make the topping, put all the ingredients in a heatproof bowl set over a saucepan of simmering water. Using an electric mixer, beat for 5–6 minutes, until the mixture is thick and softly peaking when the whisk is lifted. Swirl the topping over the cupcakes.

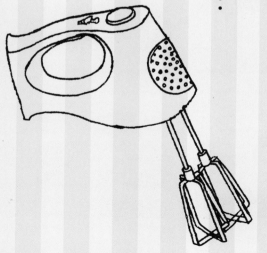

Top tip
For a fancy finish, whisk the frosting until stiff peaks form an extra few minutes and pipe on top of the cupcakes.

Peaches & Cream Cupcakes

makes 12

400 g/14 oz canned peach slices
(in fruit juice)

115 g/4 oz butter, softened

115 g/4 oz caster sugar

2 eggs, lightly beaten

115 g/4 oz self-raising flour

150 ml/5 fl oz double cream

1. Preheat the oven to 180°C/350°F/Gas Mark 4.
Put 12 paper cases in a muffin tray.

2. Drain the peaches, reserving the juice. Reserve
12 small slices and finely chop the remaining
slices.

3. Place the butter and caster sugar in a large bowl
and beat together until light and fluffy. Gradually
beat in the eggs. Sift in the flour and, using a metal
spoon, fold in gently. Fold in the chopped peaches
and 1 tablespoon of the reserved juice.

4. Spoon the mixture into the paper cases. Bake in
the preheated oven for 25 minutes, or until risen,
golden and firm to the touch. Transfer to a wire
rack and leave to cool.

5. Whip the cream until holding soft peaks. Using
a small palette knife, spread the cream over the
cupcakes. Top with the reserved peach slices.

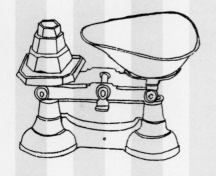

Sticky Date & Toffee Cupcakes

makes 6

85 g/3 oz dried stoned dates, chopped

½ tsp bicarbonate of soda

100 ml/3½ fl oz water

85 g/3 oz butter, softened, plus extra for greasing

85 g/3 oz soft dark brown sugar

1 tsp vanilla extract

2 eggs, lightly beaten

115 g/4 oz self-raising flour

clotted cream, to serve

toffee sauce

85 g/3 oz soft dark brown sugar

55 g/2 oz butter

4 tbsp double cream

1. Put the dates, bicarbonate of soda and water in a small saucepan and bring to the boil. Remove from the heat and set aside to cool.

2. Preheat the oven to 180°C/350°F/Gas Mark 4. Grease 6 x 150-ml/5-fl oz ovenproof ramekins.

3. Place the butter, brown sugar and vanilla extract in a large bowl and beat together until light and fluffy. Gradually beat in the eggs. Sift in the flour and, using a metal spoon, fold into the mixture followed by the date mixture.

4. Spoon the mixture into the ramekins. Put the teacups or ramekins on a baking sheet. Bake in the preheated oven for 20–25 minutes, or until risen and firm to the touch.

5. To make the toffee sauce, put all the ingredients in a small saucepan and heat until the butter has melted. Simmer for 5 minutes, stirring occasionally. Using a skewer, prick a few holes in each warm cupcake and drizzle over some of the sauce. Top with a little clotted cream and serve with the remaining toffee sauce.

Warm Molten-centred Chocolate Cupcakes

makes 8

85 g/3 oz self-raising flour

1 tbsp cocoa powder

55 g/2 oz butter, softened

55 g/2 oz caster sugar

1 large egg

55 g/2 oz plain chocolate

icing sugar, for dusting

1. Preheat the oven to 190°C/375°F/Gas Mark 5. Put 8 paper cases in a bun tray.

2. Sift the flour and cocoa powder into a large bowl. Add the butter, caster sugar and egg and, using an electric mixer, beat together until smooth.

3. Spoon half of the mixture into the paper cases. Using a teaspoon, make an indentation in the centre of each. Break the chocolate into 8 equal-sized squares and place a piece in each indentation, then spoon the remaining cake mixture on top.

4. Bake in the preheated oven for 20 minutes, or until risen and firm to the touch. Leave the cupcakes in the tin for 2–3 minutes before serving warm, dusted with icing sugar.

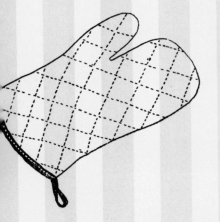